# The South African Illustrated Cookbook

Lehla Eldridge

Struik Publishers
(a division of New Holland Publishing (South Africa) (Pty) Ltd)
Cornelis Struik House
80 McKenzie Street
Cape Town 8001
South Africa
www.struik.co.za
Log on to our photographic website www.imagesofafrica.co.za for an African experience

New Holland Publishing is a member of the Johnnic Publishing Group

First Published in 2002

10 9 8 7 6 5 4

PUBLISHING MANAGER: Linda de Villiers
EDITOR: Cecilia Barfield
ILLUSTRATOR: Lehla Eldridge
CONCEPT DESIGNER: Petal Palmer
DESIGNER: Beverley Dodd
DESIGN ASSISTANT: Sean Robertson
PROOFREADER AND INDEXER: Pat Barton

ISBN: 1 86872 718 1

# contents

# Author's acknowledgements

I would like to thank the following people: Melissa, Richard and the Brake boys (for all their help and support); Jon Stokes (for helping me find recipes and for making me laugh); Linzi Rabinowitz (for all her kindness and for letting me use her computer and making me great salads); Aunty Bluma; Caitlin Ferraz (for always being so kind and for lending me her car); Peter and Almary Ferraz; Rose Gaines and Peggy Botham; Khutemba (for helping me with African cooking); Brian and Nontobeko; Lutfia Boran (for her endless patience with me when I was constantly quizzing her); Jiggy Thorne; Jon Mitchell (for daring me to go to the publishers in the first place); Karen Dudley (for teaching me a lot about South African cooking); Mama Manzi; Jeannette Crous and Mrs Beukes in Barrydale; Marlene George; Peter-Dirk Uys, Monique Weschta, Aunt Elaine, Nashen Moodley and Leslie Swart; Hein Walkinshaw and the Woodmead School ladies, Vern O'Rian, Valerie Diesel and Hazel Krige; Pat Fritchen-Pryce; Lungi Kobus-Khaye and Vathiswa Manyisane; Noor Ibrahim from the District Six Museum; Kairoonnisa Yacoob; José, Claudia and Hoffie; Khalid Jilani and Ian Alleman; Faiga of Simply Spice in Cape Town; special thanks to Miki Redelinghuys, and Stephanie; Flora Meyer; Linda, Beverley and Cecilia of Struik Publishers; my Mum (for her cooking skills and help), Dad (for his painting skills and support); Rucha (for being my brilliant sister); and anybody else whom I have forgotten to mention.

*Lehla Eldridge*

*This book is dedicated to my friends, my family, Bert and baby Evie.*

# Explanatory notes

MEASURES AND WEIGHTS:

1 kg = 2 lb 3 oz (rounded off)

100 g = 3.5 oz (rounded off)

1 litre = 1 pint 15 fl oz (rounded off)

250 ml = 9 fl. oz (rounded off)

CAKE FLOUR: equivalent to plain flour

PAWPAW: another name for papaya

SNOEK: an oily fish not unlike mackerel

BREDIE: a stew

PEPPADEW: a piquant member of the capsicum family

NAARTJIE: citrus fruit very similar to tangerine

SOSATIES: kebabs

BRAAI: the South Arican term for barbeque

MEALIE MEAL: also known as corn meal or maize meal

SAMP: consists of coarsely crushed maize kernels

# Introduction

I was raised in England and my first memories of anything South African were visits from sun-kissed relatives and blue airmail letters for my Mum; the connection with South Africa always seemed far away and remote.

In 1995 I was awarded a scholarship to study theatre in South Africa for nine months. I spent the time travelling around, working with various theatre companies and it was then that I felt a real attraction to this country. Since then I have been back and forth, and when in Europe, I find the colours, space and richness of South Africa on my mind. That, and a friend who said I would never have the guts to do it, inspired me to approach publishers with an idea for a book.

Convinced that nothing would come of it, I received a call early one morning while rehearsing for a play in England, 'Lehla, I'm from Struik, we would like you to do the book.' I was thrilled; I would be returning to South Africa and would be able to explore this vast country through the eyes of people of different cultures.

My culinary travels have taken me all over and I have met amazing people, with incredible stories. I have been so moved by their willingness to share recipes, ways of cooking, secret tips and stories and I feel privileged to have entered so many lives and kitchens. All the illustrations have sprung from things that I have seen around me, and the recipes are from the people of South Africa. In passing on these recipes I have tried to do so faithfully – as they were given to me. But if there is the odd extra dash of oil, or pinch of pepper, please forgive me. I have cooked all these dishes and they are delicious.

I want to thank everybody who has helped me to compile this book. I hope you enjoy preparing these meals as much as I do and that they will bring a little of South Africa into your home, wherever it may be!

*Lehla Eldridge*
Cape Town
2002

LEFT: *Me, at work.*

Soups and
Starters

# Hazel's Chicken Liver Pâté

SERVES 6 (GENEROUSLY)

Preparation time: 30 minutes

Setting time: 2 hours

*Thanks to Hazel Krige from Woodmead School for this Jewish recipe.*

450 g chicken livers, chopped
1 large onion, chopped
150 g mushrooms or aubergines, chopped
1 clove garlic, finely chopped
1 bay leaf
a sprig parsley, finely chopped
1 t (5 ml) dried thyme
200 g butter
salt and pepper, to taste
3 T (45 ml) brandy

Fry the chicken livers, onion, mushrooms or aubergines, garlic, bay leaf, parsley and thyme in 60 g of butter. When cooked, remove the bay leaf, add a little salt and pepper, and then the brandy. Place all the ingredients, including the remainder of the butter, in a liquidizer and blend until smooth. Transfer the mixture into a dish. Once it is cool enough, refrigerate the pâté and leave it to set.

It is delicious with crackers, and also with a smidgen of dried fruit chutney.

**LEFT:** *The Johannesburg skyline.*

# Nontobeko's Steam Bread

SERVES 4

Preparation time: 15 minutes
Cooking time: 20 minutes

*This is a traditional Xhosa recipe.*

5 cups (600 g) cake flour
1 sachet instant yeast
3 T (45 ml) white sugar
1 t (5 ml) salt
1½ cups (375 ml) warm water
1 T (15 ml) sunflower oil or olive oil
1 T (15 ml) butter, for greasing the loaf tin
boiling water

Sieve the flour and combine it with the yeast, sugar and salt. Add the warm water and the oil. Knead this into a dough and divide it into two, forming each into a ball. Place each ball into a greased mixing bowl. Leave the dough to rise for an hour in a warm place, covered with a damp tea towel. Once it has risen, punch back each piece and knead again, place it in a greased loaf tin, then leave to rise once more.

After the dough has risen, place one of the tins in a large, covered pan with just enough boiling water to reach half way up the tin. Leave covered and simmer for 20 minutes (or until a knife immersed in the dough comes out clean). Turn the loaf out onto a cooling rack. Repeat with the other tin, or freeze for later use.

The best way to enjoy this bread is to eat it while it is still warm, spread with butter.

# Butternut Soup

SERVES 3–4

Preparation time: 20 minutes

Cooking time: 20 minutes

*This delicious soup comes from a friend called Monique who lives on the Wild Coast of South Africa in a tiny place called Coffee Bay. It is claimed that a boat carrying coffee to South Africa crashed against the shore at this point. To this day, I hear that you can still find coffee trees growing there.*

1 large onion, peeled and chopped

3 T (45 ml) olive oil or 2 T (30 ml) butter

a handful fresh coriander leaves (about 7 g)

1 t (5 ml) ground cinnamon

½ T (7.5 ml) mild curry powder

2 Granny Smith apples, peeled and chopped

500 g butternut, diced

2 cups (500 ml) chicken or vegetable stock

2 cups (500 ml) milk (or 1 cup (250 ml) milk and 1 cup (250 ml) plain yoghurt)

2 T (30 ml) fresh cream (optional)

Brown the onion in the olive oil or butter, add the coriander (save a few sprigs for garnish), cinnamon and curry powder. Next, add the apples and butternut and stir for a few minutes so that all the ingredients absorb the flavours.

Add the chicken or vegetable stock, turning up the heat a little to soften the apple and butternut. Cover with a lid and leave to cook for about 10 minutes.

Once the ingredients have softened, add the milk (or half milk, half yoghurt) and leave for another 5 minutes. If desired, you may add cream and stir. Purée the soup until smooth.

Serve in bowls with a sprig of coriander.

# Cold Cucumber Soup

### SERVES 4
#### Preparation time: 20 minutes

*I have to thank the ladies who compiled the* Good Eating from Woodmead School *cookery book.*
*This is a wonderful collection of South African recipes and was given to me years ago by a friend.*
*So thank you Hazel Krige for this lovely English soup.*

1 large English cucumber, peeled and chopped
1½ cups (375 ml) cream
juice of ½ lemon
½ cup (125 ml) plain yoghurt
5 drops Tabasco sauce
6 sprigs mint
1 clove garlic, peeled
salt and pepper, to taste
fresh chives, chopped, to garnish
a pinch cayenne pepper, to garnish

Place the cucumber, cream, lemon juice, yoghurt, Tabasco sauce, sprigs of mint and garlic into a liquidizer and blend until smooth. Add salt and pepper to taste.

Serve chilled in bowls and garnish with chopped chives and a sprinkle of cayenne pepper.

**LEFT:** *A farmstall near Stellenbosch, Western Cape.*

# Spicy Lentil and Bacon Soup

SERVES 6

Preparation time: 15 minutes

Cooking time: 20 minutes

*This tasty English soup is from my Aunt Elaine in KwaZulu-Natal and is her favourite.*

225 g streaky bacon
350 g red lentils
50 g butter
3 large onions, peeled and thinly sliced
1 t (5 ml) mild curry powder
6 cups (1.5 litres) chicken stock
salt and pepper, to taste

Snip the bacon into small pieces, discarding the rind (use scissors, it makes it easier!). Place the lentils in a sieve and rinse with cold water. Melt the butter in a large saucepan. Add the bacon and cook over a gentle heat until fat from the bacon starts to run. Stir occasionally.

Stir in the onions, increase the heat and cook until the onions begin to brown. Add the curry powder and lentils and stir for a few minutes. Pour in the chicken stock and bring the soup to the boil. Add salt and pepper. Cover the pan and leave to simmer for about 15 minutes or until the lentils are soft.

# Peggy's Mealie Bread

MAKES 2 SMALL LOAVES
Preparation time: 10 minutes
Cooking time: 1½ hours

*This traditional Xhosa/Zulu recipe was given to me by a friend's mother, Peggy, from Durban. She has been cooking for years and has used this recipe ever since she can remember. It is my favourite bread.*

2 eggs
½ cup (125 ml) milk
1 x 410 g tin cream-style sweetcorn
250 g mealie meal
250 g cake flour
1 T (15 ml) baking powder
a pinch salt
2 T (30 ml) sugar
boiling water

Beat the eggs, milk and sweetcorn together. Sift in the mealie meal, cake flour, baking powder, salt and sugar, and mix. Pour the mixture into two greased bread loaf tins. Cover the tins with foil and secure with string. (You can cook them without string but it secures the foil a little better.)

Place the tins into a large saucepan that has been filled with about 5 cm of boiling water (or you can use two separate saucepans). Cover the saucepan and steam the bread over a moderate heat. To test if the bread is done, insert a knife in it – it should be clean when removed.

# *Salads*

The Bijou, an old cinema in Observatory, Cape Town.

# Peter's Peppadew and Pasta Salad

SERVES 4–6

Preparation time: 15–20 minutes

Cooking time: 15 minutes

*Last year I saw a brilliant show called 'Play with Your Food'. It was a fantastic evening. In addition to a hilarious performance, the audience was fed delicious treats throughout the show. One dish stayed in my mind and Peter Hayes has kindly given me the recipe. He now runs a wonderful restaurant in Cape Town called 'Gorgeous'. This recipe was inspired by Jill Dupleix's 'Pasta with Olives and Ham', New Food, 1994, p45 (Mitchell Beazley), but Peter has given it a New South African lilt and it is delicious hot or cold.*

250 g button mushrooms, thickly sliced

4 T (60 ml) olive oil

1 t (5 ml) Dijon mustard

500 g pasta (penne or farfalle)

1 cup (250 ml) pitted and sliced black olives

1 cup (250 ml) sliced sun dried tomatoes

15 peppadews, sliced

4 T (60 ml) Italian artichokes, drained

1 cup (250 ml) grated pecorino
   or Parmesan cheese

4 t (20 ml) fresh thyme (leaves only)

finely grated zest of 2 lemons

2 T (30 ml) lemon juice

salt and freshly ground pepper, to taste

5 or 6 basil leaves

Brown the mushrooms over a medium heat in 1 T (15 ml) olive oil and add the Dijon mustard. Cook for a few minutes until crunchy. Cook the pasta in boiling water until 'al dente' (still slightly chewy). You can prepare the rest of the ingredients while the pasta is cooking.

Once the pasta is cooked, drain the water. Over a low heat add the remaining olive oil, mushrooms in the Dijon sauce, olives, sun dried tomatoes, peppadews, artichokes, pecorino or Parmesan cheese, thyme, lemon zest, lemon juice, and salt and pepper, to taste. Mix well and keep it warm. Tear the basil leaves gently with your fingers and sprinkle them over each serving.

# Linzi's Pawpaw, Avocado and Baby Spinach Salad

SERVES 4

Preparation time: 20 minutes

Cooking time: 45 minutes

*This is a lovely New South African salad with a great dressing from Linzi, a fantastic cook.*

1 large pawpaw or 2 mangoes, peeled, pitted and sliced
2 avocados, peeled, pitted and sliced
100 g baby spinach or watercress, shredded
½ cup (125 ml) roasted pine nuts

DRESSING

2 T (30 ml) buttermilk
1 t (5 ml) wholegrain mustard
1 T (15 ml) olive oil
1 T (15 ml) lemon juice
½ t (2.5 ml) runny honey
salt and ground black pepper, to taste

Place the pawpaw or mangoes in a salad bowl. Add the avocados, spinach or watercress and the pine nuts.

To make the dressing, mix the buttermilk, mustard, olive oil, lemon juice and honey together. Add salt and pepper to taste. Pour the dressing over the salad immediately before serving.

# Sousboontjies (Sauced Beans)

*Sousboontjies, a traditional Afrikaans mealtime favourite, are usually stored in jars and eaten as a side dish, to go with a braai or with salads.*

500 g dried white kidney beans, soaked in water overnight

½ cup (125 ml) white sugar

½ cup (125 ml) grape vinegar

salt and pepper, to taste

Rinse the beans under a cold tap, place them in a saucepan and cover with water. Gently cook them over a low heat for about 2 hours. Skim off any foam that appears on the surface of the water. You may need to keep replenishing the water as it progresses. After about an hour the beans will become soft and sauce-like. When this happens, stir in the sugar and the vinegar, and add salt and pepper to taste. Depending on their age, the beans sometimes take longer but overnight soaking helps speed up the cooking process.

# FARM FRESH

# GREEN BEANS

# Feta and Green Bean Salad

SERVES 4

Preparation time: 15 minutes

Cooking time: 5–7 minutes

*Here is another New South African recipe given to me by Karen Dudley, who is an absolute genius in the kitchen. This simple, quick but impressive salad is crunchy and very tasty.*

400 g whole green beans, topped and tailed

150 g feta cheese

1 clove garlic, crushed

4 T (60 ml) olive oil

2 T (30 ml) balsamic vinegar

salt and pepper, to taste

Blanch the green beans in boiling water for 5–7 minutes. You can judge when they are ready; they should be crunchy and soft at the same time. Remove from heat and run them under cold water to stop them cooking any further. Once cool, place the beans in a salad bowl and crumble in the feta cheese. Add the garlic and drizzle in the oil and vinegar. Add salt and pepper to taste. Mix well with salad servers. Serve hot or cold.

**LEFT:** *A farm sign, outside the farmstall near Stellenbosch.*

# Roasted Sweet Potato, Fennel and Carrot Salad

SERVES 4

Preparation time: 20 minutes

Cooking time: 30 minutes

*This New South African dish is from my friend Flora. It may be served hot or cold.*

4 sweet potatoes, scrubbed and cubed
½ cup (125 ml) olive oil
2 fennel bulbs, sliced
4 carrots, grated (on the largest blade) into strips
4 T (60 ml) balsamic vinegar
salt and pepper, to taste

Place the sweet potatoes on a flat tray and pour over a ¼ cup (60 ml) of olive oil or enough to roast them nicely. Pop them in the oven at 180 °C for 30 minutes or until they're golden and crispy.

When the potatoes have been in the oven for approximately 20 minutes, place the fennel and carrots under a grill for about 10 minutes on a medium heat. You may pour a little olive oil over these if you like.

Once all the vegetables are ready, put them in a bowl and add the balsamic vinegar, the leftover olive oil, and salt and pepper to taste.

# Hot Beetroot and Garlic Salad

SERVES 4

Preparation time: 10 minutes

Cooking time: 35–40 minutes

*This delicious English recipe was given to me by Valerie Diesel of Johannesburg.*

30 cloves garlic

4 T (60 ml) olive oil

12 large beetroots, peeled

½ t (2.5 ml) salt

½ t (2.5 ml) white sugar

a handful fresh parsley, finely chopped

½ t (2.5 ml) balsamic vinegar

ground black pepper

Place the garlic cloves (unpeeled), into a roasting tray or dish and toss in olive oil. Bake them in the oven at 180 °C for about 15 minutes or until they are golden.

Boil the beetroots for 35 minutes or until soft. Once they are cooked, drain and chop them into strips and place them in a bowl. Remove the garlic from the oven and leave to cool for a minute, then peel with your fingers; the cloves pop out quite easily. Add them to the dish with the beetroot and mix in the salt, sugar, parsley, vinegar and black pepper.

This dish is best served warm, so you may want to return it to the oven for a few minutes.

Fish

# Karen's Grilled Line Fish with Gourmet Smoortjie

SERVES 5–6

Preparation time 15 minutes

Cooking time: 1 hour

*This wonderful New South African gourmet meal originates from my 'master chef' friend, Karen.*

5–6 pieces (750–900 g) fish (such as Cape Salmon, Yellowtail, Kingklip, Butterfish)

4 T (60 ml) olive oil

salt and pepper, to taste

a pinch dried origanum

GOURMET SMOORTJIE

1 kg baby onions, peeled

5 T (75 ml) olive oil

1 t (5 ml) dried thyme

1 kg small tomatoes (a cherry/yellow/plum mix)

½ T (7.5 ml) brown sugar

½ cup (125 ml) balsamic vinegar

1–2 fresh bay leaves

salt and pepper, to taste

½ handful basil leaves or chopped parsley

Par grill the fish in a pan: cook for 3 minutes on each side. Season with salt, pepper and origanum.

Place the onions in a dish, pour olive oil over and sprinkle with thyme. Roast until soft (± 25 minutes in a hot oven). Put the tomatoes in the oven 10 minutes after the onions, in a separate dish. Do not prick them (let them pop). Sprinkle sugar over the tomatoes and add 4 T (60 ml) olive oil. Cook for 15–20 minutes. Keep tossing the onions, do not allow them to dry out. When the tomatoes and onions are ready they must look caramelized. Toss them in a flattish, ovenproof dish with 1 T (15 ml) olive oil, balsamic vinegar and bay leaves. Season well with salt and pepper. Arrange the fish in the 'smoortjie' and bake at 180 °C for another 20 minutes. Spoon some of the cooking juices liquid from the onions and tomatoes over the fish and sprinkle with basil or chopped parsley.

**LEFT:** *One morning at Hout Bay, Cape Town, a man gave me advice on one of my pictures. I took it.*

25

# Lutfia's Fish Bobotie

SERVES 4–6

Preparation time: 20 minutes

Cooking time: 25 minutes

*This is a traditional Cape Malay recipe from The Bo-Kaap in Cape Town.*

2 thick slices stale white bread
½ cup (125 ml) milk
2 onions, finely chopped
2½ t (12.5 ml) butter
2 T (30 ml) white sugar
2 t (10 ml) curry powder
1 t (5 ml) turmeric
600 g white fish, such as Hake, minced or finely chopped
75 g seedless raisins
1½ T (22.5 ml) fresh lemon juice
1 t (5 ml) salt
a pinch pepper
1 cup (250 ml) milk
2 eggs
fresh lemon leaves or bay leaves

Preheat the oven to 180 °C. Soak the bread in milk, then squeeze out all the excess liquid, until the bread is quite dry.

Fry the onions in butter, add the sugar, curry powder and turmeric and fry over a medium heat until golden brown. Add the bread, fish, raisins, lemon juice, salt and pepper, and mix lightly. The fish need not be cooked for long – just brown it for a few minutes, then turn off the heat.

Beat the milk and eggs together and add half to the fish mixture. Place this in a greased ovenproof dish. Pour the rest of the milk and egg mixture over the fish. Tuck in the lemon or bay leaves and bake for 20–25 minutes until set and golden brown.

Serve warm with a salad or rice.

# Pickled Fish

SERVES 4–5

Preparation time: 15 minutes

Cooking time: 10 minutes

*This is another Cape Malay favourite from the Bo-Kaap, Cape Town. Thanks Lutfia!*

## MARINADE

1½ T (22.5 ml) turmeric
1 T (15 ml) pickle masala
1 T (15 ml) medium curry powder
4 t (20 ml) chopped root ginger
4 t (20 ml) chopped, fresh garlic
7 whole cloves
1½ cups (375 ml) brown vinegar
1 cup (250 ml) cold water
¾ cup (185 ml) white sugar
1 t (5 ml) salt
1 kg onions, peeled and sliced

## COATING FOR FISH

1 kg fish (Yellowtail or stock fish such as Hake),
   cut into smallish pieces
2 t (10 ml) turmeric
2 T (30 ml) fish masala
1 T (15 ml) chopped root ginger
1 T (15 ml) chopped, fresh garlic
a pinch salt
2 T (30 ml) sunflower oil

Put the turmeric, masala, curry powder, ginger, garlic and cloves into a saucepan. Add the vinegar, water, sugar and salt, simmer over a medium to low heat and add the onions. Cook for about 10 minutes or until the onions are crunchy.

In the meanwhile, rub the fish in a mixture of turmeric, masala, ginger, garlic and salt. Fry the fish quickly in oil over a medium to high heat for a few minutes on each side, until the fish flakes easily. Remove from heat and place in the marinade.

This dish is best served cold, with bread and butter. It may be kept for up to two months in pickle jars.

# Yzerfontein White Mussel Pasta Sauce

SERVES 6–8

Preparation time: 6 hours if using freshly picked mussels, 10 minutes for frozen

Cooking time: 30 minutes

*This recipe is from Lesley Swart. To collect mussels from Yzerfontein you require a permit and numbers are limited to 50 per person. According to Lesley, picking involves the Yzerfontein wiggle as the water up the West Coast is icy (the cold Benguela current). Wait for low tide, wade in up to your thighs and explore the sandy bottom with your toes. If you can remember the 'Twist', that is the action. Plunge your arm in and retrieve the mussels, preferably not when a wave is breaking. Transfer your quota of mussels to a bucket of sea water while you thaw out. They should stand for approximately 6 hours in sea water. If planning a visit, go in August or September, when all the flowers are out. From Yzerfontein you can also visit Evita Bezuidenhout in Darling and ask her about her Bobotie (page 37).*

50 white mussels

1 cup (250 ml) water, for steaming mussels

2 onions, peeled and diced

2 T (30 ml) olive oil

4 cloves garlic, crushed

6 large ripe tomatoes, skinned (in boiling water) and chopped

½ cup (125 ml) water (if necessary)

3 T (45 ml) chopped parsley

½–1 cup (125–250 ml) freshly grated Parmesan cheese

black pepper

Steam the mussels in a large pot until opened (discard unopened ones), remove the mussel meat, strain the liquid through a coffee filter and reserve for the sauce. If using frozen mussels, steam them for ± 5 minutes and do not keep the water for the sauce.

Fry the onions in olive oil over a medium heat until golden. Stir in the garlic and fry for another minute. Add the tomatoes and saved mussel liquid, or ½ cup (125 ml) water. Simmer for 25–30 minutes, stirring occasionally. Add the mussels and parsley. If required, add salt (taste to check because the mussel water is salty). Finally, add the Parmesan and black pepper.

Serve over cooked pasta shells with a sprinkling of Parmesan.

**LEFT:** *On the road to Yzerfontein.*

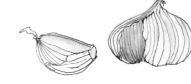

# Smoorvis Snoek

SERVES 4

Preparation time: 20 minutes

Cooking time: 20–25 minutes

*This traditional Afrikaans dish comes from Stephanie Redelinghuys in Paarl. She told me that the best thing to do after salting the fresh fish is to hang it on the washing line! I loved listening to her speak with such passion about snoek. She says never be tempted to buy a small snoek and, at the fishmongers, feel it with your fingers: if it is soft, don't touch it. It should be pink and perfect. This is a lovely, comforting recipe. I made it for her daughter, Miki, and her friend, Charl; they had not eaten it since they were children and could not stop eating it once they started.*

250 g fresh snoek
(or smoked fish, skinned, deboned and flaked)
2–3 medium potatoes, peeled and quartered
1 large onion, diced
1–2 medium tomatoes, peeled and diced
1 red or green chilli, finely chopped (optional)
250 g cooked white rice
salt and pepper, to taste

If using fresh snoek, rub the fish in salt, cut it into 'mootjies' (slices), and boil over a medium heat until tender. When cool enough, skin, debone and flake the snoek, ensuring that all the bones are removed. Set aside.

Boil the potatoes until cooked. Fry the onion, add the tomatoes, flaked fish and chilli (if desired). Add the potatoes and use a little of the water that the snoek was boiled in to moisten the mixture. Simmer for approximately 15 minutes over a low flame and serve on cooked rice. Add salt and pepper to taste.

# Fish Frikkadels (Fish Cakes)

SERVES 4

Preparation time: 20 minutes

Cooking time: 15 minutes

*Here is another Cape Malay recipe given to me by Lutfia Boran.*

100 g brown or white bread (± 5 slices)

2 cups (500 ml) milk or water

1 medium stock fish (such as Hake), deboned and minced or finely chopped

3–4 cloves garlic, crushed

1 onion, peeled and thinly sliced

1 t (5 ml) ground cumin

1 egg

½ t (2.5 ml) salt

a handful fresh coriander, chopped

a handful fresh parsley, finely chopped

1 cup (250 ml) sunflower oil

Break the bread into pieces and soak it in the milk or water. Mix the fish with the garlic, onion, cumin and egg. Add the salt. Squeeze the liquid from the bread and add the bread to the mixture, with the coriander and parsley.

Heat the oil in a frying pan over a medium flame. Roll the mixture into palm-sized flat balls (frikkadels) and place them in the hot oil. (I always had a fear of deep-frying but simply watch that the oil doesn't get too hot. Also put the frikkadels into the pan carefully, so as not to splash the oil!) Gently flip them over when they are golden brown on one side. Place some kitchen paper towel in a bowl and when the frikkadels are ready, place them on the towel to absorb excess oil.

Frikkadels are delicious with a tomato sambal (page 57) or Karen's Gourmet Smoortjie (page 25).

Mains

# Peggy's Durban Lamb Breyani

SERVES 8

Preparation time: 8 hours minimum for marinating, and another 25 minutes

Cooking time: 60–90 minutes

*This Indian dish, delicious with a dahl, involves layering the different ingredients and is actually very simple.*

MARINADE
1 T (15 ml) crushed garlic
1 T (15 ml) grated root ginger
4 x 3 cm pieces stick cinnamon
4 cardamom pods
4 allspice berries
½ T (7.5 ml) turmeric
4 whole cloves
½ T (7.5 ml) chilli powder
3 fresh green chillies
1 T (15 ml) ground coriander
1 T (15 ml) ground cumin

¾ cup (185 ml) plain yoghurt
½ cup (125 ml) lemon juice

1 kg lamb, boned, cubed, washed and patted dry
1 T (15 ml) sunflower oil
6 medium potatoes, peeled and halved
300 g cooked brown lentils
500 g Basmati rice, soaked overnight
2 onions, peeled, sliced and deep fried
5 saffron strands, soaked in 50 ml warm water
50 g cold butter
a handful fresh coriander

Mix the marinade ingredients with the lamb and refrigerate for 8 hours. Heat oil in a large pot over a low flame.
Place half the potatoes at the bottom, cover with 75 g lentils, and then with 125 g rice. Add the meat (do not wash
the marinade bowl yet), onions and the rest of the potatoes. Mix half the remaining rice in the bowl with
leftover marinade and layer it over the onions. Add half the remaining lentils. Finally, layer the
remaining rice, onions and lentils. Place saffron at the edges and dot cold butter over the top. Cover
with a tight-fitting lid and steam over a low heat for 60–90 minutes (do not remove lide for an hour).
If the breyani looks dry, add a dash of water. Sprinkle coriander on top for the last 10 minutes.

**LEFT:** *The Durban City Hall — a little girl sat with me and changed my painting water for me.*

33

# Karen's Mum's Tomato Bredie with Lamb

SERVES 4

Preparation time: 20 minutes

Cooking time: 1½–2 hours

*This Cape Malay bredie is from my friend Karen's mother, Ruthee.*

4 onions, peeled and chopped

4 T (60 ml) olive or sunflower oil

1 chicken stock cube

600 g lamb pieces (cheaper cuts are better, such as neck – 150 g per person)

1 t (5 ml) coriander seeds

1 red chilli, finely chopped

2 t (10 ml) dried mixed herbs (e.g. origanum and thyme)

4 cloves garlic, chopped

2 kg ripe tomatoes (or 4 x 410 g tins tomatoes)

1–2 T (15–30 ml) sugar

3 bay leaves

Brown the onions in a large saucepan in the oil until they are translucent and golden. (I have been told that loving your onions is the secret to Malay cooking!) Crumble in the chicken stock, then push the onions to one side in the saucepan and add the meat. If there is not enough room, put the onions in a separate dish and brown the meat in the saucepan. Place the onions back onto the meat and add the coriander seeds, chilli, dried mixed herbs and garlic. Cook for a few minutes, then stir in the tomatoes, sugar and bay leaves. Leave to simmer over a low heat for 1½–2 hours. It is delicious and well worth the wait. Serve with rice.

# Moong Dahl (Magnidhal)

SERVES 2

Preparation time: 10 minutes

Cooking time: 30–45 minutes

*This recipe, which originated in India centuries ago, was given to me by Kairoonnisa*
*in Johannesburg and it has been passed down through her family.*

1 cup (250 ml) moong dahl (split mung beans), soaked overnight in hot water or quick-soaked and boiled for 30–45 minutes over a medium heat

1 T (15 ml) crushed ginger/garlic/green chilli masala mixture (available in most spice shops) (or 1 t (5 ml) each crushed garlic and finely chopped root ginger and ½ t (2.5 ml) finely chopped green chillies)

1 t (5 ml) salt

1 t (5 ml) turmeric

1 t (5 ml) red chilli powder

1 t (5 ml) ground cumin

1 t (5 ml) ground coriander

2 green peppers, sliced (optional)

1 onion, peeled and grated or finely chopped

1 tomato, skinned and grated or finely chopped

1 cup (250 ml) water

a handful fresh coriander or 2 spring onions, finely chopped

Drain and wash the pre-soaked moong dahl. Put it in a saucepan and add the ginger, garlic, green chilli, salt, turmeric, red chilli powder, cumin, coriander, green peppers, onion and tomato. Add water and cook the dahl over a low heat for 30–45 minutes. When cooked, garnish with the fresh coriander or spring onions.

This goes well with sambals (page 57).

# Darling Evita's Dried Fruit Bobotie of Reconciliation

SERVES 6

Preparation time: 45 minutes

Cooking time: 45 minutes

*I feel very honoured to have a recipe from Evita Bezuidenhout. Anybody who makes this Cape Malay dish will be touched by her culinary magic!*

| | |
|---|---|
| 6 dried apricots | 2 t (10 ml) turmeric |
| 6 dried apple rings | 1 kg minced beef |
| ½ cup (125 ml) seedless raisins | 2 thick slices stale white bread, crumbed |
| 1 cup (250 ml) cold black tea | 3½ T (52.5 ml) vinegar |
| 2 large onions, peeled and sliced | salt and pepper, to taste |
| 1 cup (250 ml) orange juice | 4 eggs |
| 2 T (30 ml) olive oil | ½ cup (125 ml) milk |
| 1 T (15 ml) curry powder | fresh lemon leaves (optional) |

Soak the apricots, apple rings and raisins in the tea until soft. Drain the fruit, halve the apricots and cut the apple rings into pieces. Preheat the oven to 180 °C. Grease an ovenproof dish well.

Boil the onions in the orange juice until soft, drain, then fry lightly in oil.

Add curry powder, turmeric, minced beef, breadcrumbs, vinegar, salt, pepper and soaked fruit. Mix lightly with a large fork and place in the dish. Beat the eggs and milk together and pour over the mixture. Fold a few lemon leaves into triangles and tuck them into the mixture.

Bake the bobotie on the middle rack of the oven for 45 minutes, or until the egg 'custard' has set. Serve hot.

This tastes wonderful with a crunchy salad.

LEFT: *Evita Bezuidenhout and her bobotie.*

# Bunny Chow

SERVES 2

Preparation time: 10 minutes

Cooking time 20 minutes

*For those of you who are unaccustomed to this South African Indian delight, it has nothing to do with bunnies. In fact, the bunny chow recipe that I have chosen is vegetarian. I asked many people for bunny chow recipes and the general response was a giggled 'you just make it up and then fill up a loaf of bread'. I wanted to be more specific and finally Kairoonnisa, who is originally from KwaZulu-Natal, came up with this wonderful version.*

*carrot - finely chopped.*

1 onion, finely chopped

1 T (15 ml) ginger/garlic/green chilli mix

(or 1 t (5 ml) each finely chopped root ginger and garlic and

½ t (2.5 ml) finely chopped green chilli)

1 t (5 ml) ground cumin

1 t (5 ml) ground coriander

1 t (5 ml) red chilli powder

1 t (5 ml) salt

2 large ripe tomatoes, skinned and finely chopped or grated

1 cup (250 g) beans (butter or sugar), soaked overnight and cooked until soft (or 1 x 410 g tin baked beans)

1 loaf white bread, unsliced

a handful fresh coriander, finely chopped

Over a medium to high heat brown the onion in a saucepan and add the ginger, garlic, green chilli, cumin, coriander, chilli powder and salt. Let the spices cook with the onions for a few minutes until golden. Add the tomatoes and the beans. Lower the heat, cover with a lid and simmer for approximately 15 minutes.

Cut the loaf of bread in half width-wise and pull out the soft insides, leaving a 10 mm crust shell. Fill with the bean curry and garnish with fresh coriander. (You can also make a lid for your bean bunny by putting the scooped out dough on top.)

Eat with your hands, preferably sitting around a big, open fire, looking at the stars.

# Venison Pie

SERVES 4

Preparation time: 15 minutes

Cooking time: 2–3 hours

*This traditional Afrikaans recipe was kindly given to me by my friend Miki's mother, Stephanie Redelinghuys of Paarl. It's delicious!*

500 g venison
2 T (30 ml) olive oil
125 g pork or bacon, chopped in small squares
a pinch dried origanum
a pinch dried thyme
a pinch dried rosemary
a pinch dried basil
3 whole cloves

1 onion, peeled and chopped
4 T (60 ml) sago
juice of ¼ lemon
a dash Worcester sauce
400 g frozen puff pastry, thawed and rolled out
1 egg yolk
2 T (30 ml) milk

Brown the venison in olive oil in a large pot. Remove from pot and set aside. In the same pot, brown the pork or bacon, then add the venison, herbs and cloves. Cover with water and simmer on low for 2–3 hours. In a separate pan, gently fry the onion and add it to the meat. Put the sago in a bowl, cover with water and soak for 30 minutes. When the meat is cooked it should be flaky. Remove the meat from the water (save the water), place it in a dish and allow it to cool. Flake finely, removing excess fat or bones. Return the meat to the water and add the sago. Cook for 20–30 minutes until the sauce thickens and the sago is glassy. Add lemon juice and Worcester sauce to taste. Cool.

Line a greased pie dish with the puff pastry. Pour the filling into the dish and cover with another sheet of pastry. Prick the top and decorate with pastry leaves or flowers. Mix the egg yolk and milk together and brush it over the pie crust. Pop the pie into the oven and bake at 180 °C for 20 minutes, or until the pastry is golden.

Serve with quince or apple jelly.

# Lamb Potjiekos

SERVES 4–6
Preparation time: 40 minutes
Cooking time: 3 hours

*This Afrikaans stew is traditionally cooked in a 'potjie', a three-legged African cooking pot that is placed over hot coals. You can also make the dish in a large, heavy-bottomed saucepan in your kitchen. If you prefer a hot, spicy potjiekos, add more chillies and curry powder. Ian Alleman, who makes it every three months for poetry readings under the stars in Nieu Bethesda in the Great Karoo, suggests that you could use pumpkin instead of butternut, or tomatoes instead of spinach.*

4 large onions, peeled and chopped
4 T (60 ml) sunflower or olive oil
4 t (20 ml) medium curry powder
1 t (5 ml) crushed, dried naartjie peel
1 T (15 ml) ground cumin
2 red chillies, finely chopped
1 T (15 ml) ground coriander
4 curry leaves
4 bay leaves

600 g lamb neck or shank, cubed or sliced
juice of 1 lemon
4 large potatoes, peeled and chopped
4 carrots, scraped and chopped
250 g butternut, peeled and chopped
5 cloves garlic, crushed
200 g spinach
1 T (15 ml) salt

In a 'potjie', brown the onion in oil over a medium heat. Add the curry powder, naartjie peel, cumin, chillies, coriander, curry leaves and bay leaves, and sauté for a minute or so. Add the meat and brown it with the onions and spices. Pour in enough boiling water to just cover the meat, then add the lemon juice. Lower the heat and simmer. Add a layer of potatoes, followed by layers of carrot, butternut, garlic and finally spinach. Season with salt, replace the lid and leave to simmer slowly for approximately 3 hours until the meat is tender and the vegetables cooked.

Use a large spoon when dishing up and serve the stew with rice or samp and beans, pot bread and a chutney atjar.

LEFT: *The Owl House Garden at Nieu Bethesda in the Karoo.*

# Flora's Table Mountain Mushroom Fillet

SERVES 4–6

Preparation time: 15 minutes

Cooking time: 30 minutes

*Devised by my friend Flora, this New South African dish includes mushrooms found on Table Mountain.*

600–800 g fillet steak, beef or pork

1 T (15 ml) butter

sufficient mashed potato for 6 people

1 T (15 ml) balsamic vinegar

400 g green beans, topped, tailed and steamed

500 g carrots, peeled, cut into strips and steamed

SAUCE

1 T (15 ml) butter

1 onion, peeled and sliced

2 cloves garlic

4 cups (1 litre) chopped assorted mushrooms
(pine rings, *Boletus edulis*, blushers, porcini,
oyster), or a mix of button and flat mushrooms

1–2 cups (250–500 ml) red wine (Pinotage)

2 sprigs rosemary

1 t (5 ml) fresh thyme leaves

½ cube beef stock

1 t (5 ml) sugar

4 T (60 ml) cream

salt and pepper, to taste

Sear the meat in butter in a pan over a medium to high heat. Remove the meat and set it aside. To make the sauce, add a little more butter to the pan and fry the onion and garlic over a medium heat until golden. Add the mushrooms, sauté for 1 minute, then add half the wine, the rosemary and thyme. Crumble in the stock cube and sprinkle in the sugar. Lower the heat and simmer, adding more wine if the sauce looks as though it is drying out. Spread the mashed potato into a flat, ovenproof dish. Slice the fillet into discs and line them along the top of the mash. Pour the balsamic vinegar over the meat. Bake in the oven at 220 °C for ± 10 minutes.

Check the sauce; at the very end you can add cream, salt and pepper. Take the meat out of the oven and arrange the carrots and beans at either end of the dish. Pour the sauce over the meat and serve.

# Sosaties

MAKES 14–16

Preparation time: 25 minutes, then overnight in refrigerator

Cooking time: 20–30 minutes

*To make this well-loved Cape Malay/Afrikaans dish you may have to search for all the spices. Luckily, in Cape Town there is a wonderful shop called Wellington Fruit Growers that stocks every spice imaginable. I recently discovered that my family owned a grocery shop at the same address many years ago, so I feel quite proud when I visit it. If you can't find all these spices, do your best with what you have. Thanks once again to Lutfia for this recipe.*

4 large onions, finely sliced

4 T (60 ml) sunflower or olive oil

2–3 T (30–45 ml) tamarind (seedless paste)

½ cup (125 ml) boiling water

2 heaped T (35 ml) brown sugar

1 t (5 ml) medium-hot curry powder

1 small chilli, finely chopped

½ T (7.5 ml) finely chopped garlic

1 t (5 ml) ground cumin

1 t (5 ml) fennel seeds

1 t (5 ml) ground coriander

1 T (15 ml) koknie (leaf) masala

1 kg beef or lamb, cut into small squares

14–16 bamboo skewers

½ cup (125 ml) boiling water

3 x 3 cm pieces stick cinnamon

3 bay leaves

5 allspice berries

4 whole cloves

Fry the onions in oil, over a medium heat, until pink. In a cup, mix the tamarind, boiling water and sugar into a paste. Add the paste, curry powder, chilli, garlic, cumin, fennel, coriander and masala to the onions. Reduce the heat and cook for 20 minutes, adding a little water if dry. Thread the meat onto skewers – ± 15 pieces each. In a dish, cover the sosaties with the marinade. Once cool, refrigerate overnight. Cook them over a low heat for 20–30 minutes, with boiling water, cinnamon, bay leaves, allspice and cloves. Alternatively, they can be coal-braaied.

They are delicious served with yellow rice (page 58) or mash.

# Pumpkin and Lamb Bredie

### SERVES 4–6
Preparation time: 20 minutes
Cooking time: 1½–2 hours

*This Cape Malay recipe was given to me by Karen Dudley.*

4 onions, peeled and chopped
4 T (60 ml) olive or sunflower oil
2 chicken stock cubes
1 t (5 ml) ground allspice
4 x 3 cm pieces stick cinnamon
2 cardamom pods
5 whole cloves
1 kg lamb cuts (e.g. neck or shank)
2 cups (500 ml) water
3 T (45 ml) honey
600-700 g pumpkin or butternut,
cut into large chunks
1 cup (250 ml) chopped fresh parsley

Brown the onions in oil in a large saucepan over a medium heat. Crumble in the stock cubes. Add the allspice, cinnamon, cardamom and cloves. Brown the lamb in a separate saucepan. Once slightly cooked, add the meat to the onions and pour in water, then add the honey. Reduce the heat and leave to simmer for 1½–2 hours; the longer you leave it the tastier it is. Add the pumpkin or butternut in the last 45 minutes of cooking time.

Serve in bowls and garnish with parsley.

**LEFT:** *A typical hairdressers' salon on the street.*

*Poultry*

# Coconut Chicken

SERVES 6

Preparation time: 40 minutes

Cooking time: 45 minutes

*This is a Cape Malay-influenced recipe from the kitchen of Karen Dudley.*

6–8 (700–800 g) deboned chicken breasts, with skin
3 T (45 ml) olive or sunflower oil
3–4 onions, peeled and chopped
3 bay leaves
5–6 cloves garlic, finely chopped
4 t (20 ml) chopped root ginger
2 red chillies
4 t (20 ml) ground coriander
4 t (20 ml) ground cumin
2 t (10 ml) mild curry powder
2 t (10 ml) turmeric

1 t (5 ml) mixed herbs
a pinch each salt and pepper
2–3 T (30–45 ml) apricot jam
1 T (15 ml) honey
4 large ripe tomatoes, skinned (or 1 x 410 g tin tomatoes)
4 x 3 cm pieces stick cinnamon
2 x 410 g tins coconut milk (or 1 x 410 g tin coconut milk and 1 x 410 g tin coconut cream)
a handful dried apricots, chopped
a handful dried apple, chopped
a handful fresh coriander, to garnish

Heat the oven to 160 °C. Brown the chicken breasts lightly in oil, over a medium heat, searing both sides for a few minutes, then transfer them to a baking dish. Brown the onions in leftover oil. Add the bay leaves, garlic, ginger and chillies and cook a little longer. Stir in the coriander, cumin, curry powder, turmeric, mixed herbs, salt and pepper, mix well and add the apricot jam and honey. By now the herbs and spices should be golden. Add the tomatoes, cinnamon, coconut milk, apricot and apple pieces. Cook for another 10 minutes and pour the mixture over the chicken. Bake for 25 minutes. The chicken may be raised and grilled for an extra 5 minutes to brown it slightly.

This is delicious served with basmati or yellow rice. Garnish with fresh coriander.

**LEFT:** *These women in KwaZulu-Natal, near Underberg, are sorting chillies and gooseberries.*

# Braai Chicken

SERVES 3

Preparation time: 10 minutes, then 3–4 hours in refrigerator

Cooking time: 15–20 minutes

*This traditional Afrikaans recipe comes from a great cook and a good friend, Hoffie.*

6 pieces (± 700 g) chicken

MARINADE
2 T (30 ml) olive oil
¾ cup (185 ml) white wine
a pinch chilli powder
1 t (5 ml) ground cumin
a large pinch black pepper
a pinch salt
½ cup (125 ml) sweet chutney
3 T (45 ml) balsamic vinegar
1–2 t (5–10 ml) Dijon mustard
2 T (30 ml) tomato sauce
2 T (30 ml) soya sauce or Worcester sauce

Place the chicken pieces in a marinade dish. In another bowl, mix the oil, wine, chilli powder, cumin, pepper, salt, chutney, vinegar, mustard, tomato sauce and soya sauce or Worcester sauce together. Pour the marinade over the chicken pieces and leave to marinate in the fridge for 3–4 hours.

When ready, braai (barbecue) your chicken over hot coals, basting with the marinade, for 15–20 minutes or until cooked.

# Rosa's Chicken Curry

Preparation time: 20 minutes

Cooking time: 1½ hours

*This is an Indian curry from my friend Rosa who is from Durban. It has been passed down in her family and is so delicious that people often have third helpings!*

5 T (75 ml) sunflower or olive oil

3 x 3 cm pieces stick cinnamon

1 large onion, peeled and sliced

3 cardamom pods

1 T (15 ml) turmeric

1 T (15 ml) ground cumin

2 t (10 ml) 'extra special' medium curry
(available in Durban, but any good-quality
medium curry powder is fine)

2 large tomatoes, peeled and grated or chopped

2 t (10 ml) crushed root ginger

2 cloves garlic, crushed

5 or 6 curry leaves

2 kg chicken pieces

1 T (15 ml) salt

1 T (15 ml) sweet chutney or honey,
mixed in ½ glass (200 ml) warm water

3 potatoes, peeled and halved

1 cup (250 ml) fresh green peas

a handful fresh coriander

Heat the oil in a large saucepan over a medium heat. Stir in the cinnamon, onion, cardamom pods, turmeric and cumin, and fry until golden. Add the curry powder, tomatoes, ginger, garlic and curry leaves, and leave to cook for about 5 minutes, then add the chicken and salt. Stir in the chutney or honey mixture. Simmer over a low heat for 50 minutes to an hour. Add the potatoes and cook for another 20 minutes, then stir in the peas. Finally, add the fresh coriander and leave it to lie on top of the curry.

This is lovely served with yellow rice (page 58) and sambals (page 57).

# Flora's Chutney Chicken

SERVES 4–6
Preparation time: 15 minutes
Cooking time: 1 hour

*This delicious Xhosa dish (with a Cape Malay influence) is incredibly quick and easy to make.*
*As Flora says, it is a wonderful family dish yet still exotic and tasty and could also be served at a dinner party.*
*So don't be put off by its simplicity, it is a winner!*

12 small potatoes, peeled
½ cup (125 ml) cake flour
1 T (15 ml) chicken stock powder
or 1 cube, crumbled
4–6 (± 500 g) chicken pieces,
washed and patted dry

1 T (15 ml) butter or olive oil
3 T (45 ml) mild curry powder
1 cup (250 ml) sweet fruit chutney
1 stock cube, dissolved in ½ cup (125 ml) water
2 cups (500 ml) milk
salt and pepper, to taste

Par boil the potatoes (while you prepare the rest) for approximately 7 minutes.

On a plate or in a flattish bowl, mix the flour and the dry chicken stock, then press the chicken pieces into the mixture until they are well coated. Melt the butter or oil in a pan over a medium to high heat and brown the chicken pieces for a few minutes on both sides. Transfer the chicken to an ovenproof dish.

Drain the potatoes and arrange them around the chicken. Mix the curry powder, chutney and dissolved stock cube in a bowl with the milk and season with salt and pepper. Mix well then pour the mixture over the chicken. Bake in the oven at 180 °C for an hour.

Serve with rice or vegetables.

**LEFT:** *My friend Anna in an apron from The Pilani Centre, Khayelitsha, Cape Town.*

# José's Pan-fried Fillets of Ostrich with Port and Cranberry Sauce

SERVES 4

Preparation time: 5 minutes

Cooking time: 20 minutes

*This is a New South African recipe for a tasty steak with a wonderful sauce.*

### SAUCE

1½ cups (375 ml) South African Pinotage

1 T (15 ml) cranberry jelly

½ cup (125 ml) port

4 t (20 ml) whole green peppercorns

6 T (90 ml) fresh cream

### STEAK

800 g ostrich steak (± 200 g per person)

1 T (15 ml) crushed black peppercorns

2 T (30 ml) olive oil

4 sprigs fresh rosemary

Pour the wine into a saucepan and bring to a boil over a medium to high heat. Stir in the cranberry jelly. Reduce heat and simmer until caramelized and sauce coats the back of a spoon. Add the port, reduce once again until the sauce is quite thick (it should drip off a spoon very slowly). Don't be alarmed as to how little sauce there is; you only need 1 T per steak. Add the green peppercorns, then add the cream to the sauce and let it reduce for a few minutes.

Cut the steaks into portions of two smallish steaks per person. Coat them with the black peppercorns, then brush with oil on one side. Heat the oil in a frying pan over a medium to high heat and when hot place the steaks, oil side down, in the pan. Brush the other top with oil. Cook the steaks quickly for 1½–2 minutes on each side (medium rare); ostrich should not be overcooked because it will become tough. Once the steaks are done, arrange them on plates, one wedged slightly on top of the other. Add the pan juices to the sauce. Pour the sauce over the steaks and decorate each with a sprig of rosemary.

Serve with a feta and green bean salad (page 21) and a hot beetroot and garlic salad (page 23).

# Trinchados

SERVES 4

Preparation time: 10 minutes

Cooking time: 45 minutes

*This dish comes from my Portuguese friend, Dominique.*

500 g chicken pieces
2 T (30 ml) olive oil
1 large onion, peeled and chopped
3 garlic cloves, chopped
1 red chilli, finely chopped
4 large tomatoes, skinned in boiling water
and chopped
2 cups (500 ml) red wine
½ T (7.5 ml) sugar or honey
1 t (5 ml) chilli paste (optional)
salt and pepper, to taste
a few sprigs fresh basil

In a pan, brown the chicken pieces in olive oil over a medium heat, then remove them to another dish on the side.

Brown the onion in the same pan until golden, then stir in the garlic and chilli. Cook for a few minutes. Add the tomatoes, wine, sugar or honey, chilli paste, salt and pepper, and cook over a medium heat for 15–20 minutes. Once the sauce has reduced sufficiently, add the chicken and cook for another 15–20 minutes. If the sauce begins to look dry, add a dash more wine.

Serve in bowls with flat Portuguese bread. Garnish with a sprig of basil.

# Guinea Fowl Pot Roast

SERVES 3–4

Preparation time: 15 minutes

Cooking time: 1 hour 40 minutes

*This New South African recipe was shown to me by Pat Pryce-Fitchen, the owner of the Zanzibar restaurant in Cape Town. She kindly took me into the kitchen and gave me a brilliant cookery lesson. This delicious dish is recommended for wintry evenings.*

1 guinea fowl (or duck)

2 large onions, peeled and sliced

1 T (15 ml) finely chopped garlic

6 small to medium carrots, peeled and chopped

1 T (15 ml) grated root ginger

4 whole star anise

2 T (30 ml) tamari or soya sauce

2 T (30 ml) sesame oil

salt and black pepper

1 cup (250 ml) apple juice

¾ cup (190) ml red wine

4 Granny Smith apples, de-cored, peeled and quartered

2 t (10 ml) salt

1 t (5 ml) black pepper

10 potatoes, peeled and quartered

½ cup (125 ml) Kalahari Thirstland liqueur (or Calvados)

Place the bird in the oven at 200 °C for 10–15 minutes, to remove excess fat.

Fry the onions, garlic, carrots, ginger, star anise and tamari in sesame oil for 5 minutes in a heavy-based saucepan. Sprinkle the bird very generously with salt and black pepper, including the inside cavity. Place the bird in the saucepan, breast side down, and brown slightly. Add the apple juice and red wine. Bring to the boil and reduce to a very low heat for 10 minutes. Add the apples. Transfer all to an ovenproof dish and bake at 180 °C for 1 hour.

Remove from the oven, add the salt, pepper and potatoes and oven bake for a further 25 minutes. Finally, stir in the Kalahari liqueur or Calvados.

Serve with basmati rice.

**LEFT:** *Ouma Ossewania's Kitchen at Evita se Perron in Darling.*

*Side dishes*

# *Sambals*

SERVES 4

Preparation time: 30 minutes

*I remember my Mum making this for me when I was younger and I now realize how much I was influenced by South African food as a child. I used to find it exciting to have various little piles of different food around the side of my plate. Here are three simple sambal options of Cape Malay/Indian origin, which are delicious with curries and hot food.*

### OPTION 1

1 large juicy red tomato, skinned and chopped into small pieces
1 medium onion, peeled and finely chopped
1 dash lemon juice
1 t (5 ml) white sugar
4 T (60 ml) fresh coriander, finely chopped
salt and pepper, to taste

Mix the tomato and onion together in a bowl, add the lemon juice, sugar and fresh coriander. Season well with salt and pepper.

### OPTION 2

50 g desiccated coconut

That is it. Put the coconut in a bowl and sprinkle it onto curry.

### OPTION 3

2 bananas, sliced
½ cup (125 ml) Greek yoghurt
4 T (60 ml) fresh coriander, chopped
1 dash lemon juice
salt, to taste

In a bowl, gently mix bananas with the yoghurt and coriander. Squeeze in a dash of lemon juice and add a sprinkle of salt. (Bananas on their own are also good.)

**LEFT:** *My favourite shop, Wellington's, Darling Street, Cape Town.*

# Yellow Rice

SERVES 6
Preparation time: 5 minutes
Cooking time: 20 minutes

*This is a traditional Cape Malay favourite.*

3 cups (750 ml) basmati rice
1 t (5 ml) turmeric
½ cup (125 ml) raisins
2 x 3 cm pieces stick cinnamon
2 onions, peeled and finely chopped
4 T (60 ml) desiccated coconut (optional)
salt and pepper, to taste

Place the rice in a saucepan and cover with water. (The secret to boiling rice is to double the amount of water to the amount of rice, so, if the rice is a 4 cm high in the pan add 8 cm of water.) Add the turmeric, raisins and cinnamon, and simmer until the rice is cooked (approximately 15 minutes) but not soggy. Sauté the onions in a separate pan until they are golden. Once the rice is cooked, drain, then stir in the onions and coconut, if desired. Season well with salt and pepper.

# Langebaan Cinnamon Pumpkin

SERVES 2

Preparation time: 10 minutes

Cooking time: 25 minutes

*This traditional Afrikaans recipe is a simple but tasty side dish that I discovered in Langebaan on the Cape West Coast of South Africa. It may also be served as a pudding by omitting the butter and salt, and adding fresh cream instead.*

500 g pumpkin, peeled and chopped

1 T (15 ml) sugar

½ T (7.5 ml) ground cinnamon

1 t (5 ml) butter

a pinch salt (optional)

(or 1 T (15 ml) cream, then omit butter and salt)

Place pumpkin in a saucepan and partially cover with water. Add the sugar and cinnamon and boil until the pumpkin is soft. Drain, then mash the pumpkin with the butter. Add salt if necessary.

Serve this dish with any main course – it goes well with bobotie (page 37) – or as a pudding in small dishes with a dollop of cream and a dusting of ground cinnamon.

# Mfino Spinach

SERVES 4–6
Preparation time: 10 minutes
Cooking time: 10 minutes

*This is a traditional dish that was given to me by Lungi Kobus-Khaye and Vathiswa Manyisane
at a great Xhosa restaurant called 'Masande' in Crossroads, Cape Town.*

1 onion, finely chopped
2 T (30 ml) olive or sunflower oil
½ cabbage, finely chopped
2 bunches spinach (600 g), chopped
a pinch salt

Brown the onion in the oil in a large saucepan over a medium heat. Stir in the cabbage. Cook until it is tender. Add the spinach and a pinch of salt. Cover the saucepan, lower the heat and leave it to simmer for a few minutes.

Serve hot or cold.

**LEFT:** *A car repair shop in Guguletu Township.*

# Mama Manzi's Mealie Pap

*Thank you Mama Manzi for this recipe (of Zulu/Xhosa/Venda/Pedi origin).*

3 cups (750 ml) water
a pinch salt
1 cup (250 ml) mealie meal
10 g butter

In a saucepan, bring the water to a boil. Add the salt and mealie meal while stirring very briskly, preferably with a whisk. As soon as the mealie meal turns into a rough-textured paste, cover it and lower the heat. Leave to cook for approximately 30 minutes, stirring every 3–4 minutes. Don't be concerned if the 'pap' sticks to the pan, as it is easy to wash off. When ready, it will be like a smooth paste, then add butter.

This goes well with Mfino Spinach (page 61), any curry or potjiekos dish.

# Mama Manzi's Samp and Beans

SERVES 6–8
Preparation time: 5 minutes
Cooking time: 2½–3hrs

*This Xhosa/Zulu recipe was given to me by Mutu Manzi, a great cook. I followed her around the kitchen while she taught me how to make traditional Samp and Beans. Although I cannot speak Afrikaans, I quickly learnt the words 'rou' (raw) and 'proe' (taste) that morning.*

1½ cups (375 ml) dried kidney beans, picked over and preferably soaked overnight
1 cup (250 ml) samp, rinsed
5 carrots, peeled and diced

3 chicken stock cubes
1 t (5 ml) medium curry powder
2 potatoes, peeled and chopped
2 tomatoes, skinned and chopped

If you don't soak the beans overnight, you will need to increase the cooking time. Wash the beans in a sieve under cold water. Put them in a large saucepan with the samp and cover with water (about 2–3 cm higher than the beans). Do not put salt in the water, as it will make the beans tough. Cover and leave to cook over a medium to low heat for 2½–3 hours. Top up the water if it begins to look dry.

After 2½ hours (when the samp and beans are nearly ready), add the carrots and leave to cook for approximately 10 minutes. Crumble in the stock cubes and curry powder, then add the potatoes and finally the tomatoes. When the beans are soft, they are ready.

This is a great dish for a winter's day and can be served with pap (page 62) and Mfino spinach (page 61).

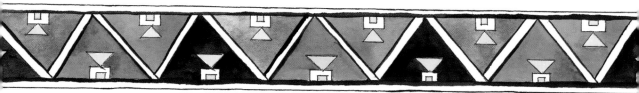

Desserts

# Sweet Chana Maghuj

MAKES 16 SMALL PIECES
Preparation time: 25 minutes
Setting time: overnight

*This Indian dish was kindly given to me by Khalid Jilani, who has an incredible sweetmeat shop in Victoria Street, Durban, called 'Makkah'. He told me that he has never revealed a recipe before, so I feel very fortunate and honoured. Khalid also said that if I wanted to make any of his other recipes I would have to train in his shop for three months! Thank you Khalid, I am grateful for this wonderful sweetmeat recipe.*

400 g butter (or 250 g butter ghee)     5 g ground cardamom (grind the pods in a blender)
250 g chick pea flour/chana flour      125 g almonds, roughly chopped
100 g milk powder            250 g icing sugar

Make the ghee first, unless, of course, you already have it. Do not be discouraged as it is easy. Put the butter in a saucepan and leave it to boil gently for about 10 minutes. Scoop off the foam that rises to the top and pour out the clear butter (ghee), leaving behind the layer of salt at the bottom of the pan.

Mix the ghee and the flour together in a saucepan over a low heat for approximately 20 minutes. The flour will give off a distinctive odour when ready. Add the milk powder, cardamom and almonds. Mix well and continue cooking for another 5 minutes.

A tip from Khalid is to remove the saucepan from the stove and put it on the floor. Mix in the icing sugar. This takes some elbow grease and the floor provides a solid surface.

Transfer the mixture to a tray and press it down quite firmly. Leave it to cool and it will be ready the next day. Cut into small slices and serve.

**LEFT:** *Bo-Kaap, Cape Town. Sketched while sitting on the pavement and nearly having a car run over my feet.*

# Pumpkin Fritters

SERVES 10–12

Preparation time: 10–15 minutes

Cooking time: 15–20 minutes

*This is another traditional South African recipe from Evita se Perron, for which
I would like to thank Evita Bezuidenhout and Marlene George.*

### FRITTERS

500 g pumpkin, skinned, seeded and cubed
a pinch salt
water, to cover pumpkin
1 egg, lightly beaten
250 g cake flour
1 t (5 ml) baking powder
a pinch ground cinnamon
1–2 T (15–30 ml) vegetable oil

### SYRUP

125 g brown sugar
½ cup (125 ml) water
1 t (5 ml) cornflour

### CINNAMON SUGAR

2 t (10 ml) ground cinnamon
½ cup (125 ml) sugar

Cook the pumpkin in a little salted water over medium heat until soft. Drain and mash with the egg, flour, baking powder and cinnamon. Heat a little vegetable oil in a frying pan and drop in spoonfuls of the batter. Fry the fritters on both sides until golden.

For the syrup, combine the sugar, water and cornflour in a small saucepan and bring to the boil, slowly stirring until the sugar dissolves. Boil briskly until thick and syrupy. Pour the syrup over the fritters, then sprinkle with cinnamon sugar, made by mixing cinnamon and sugar.

# Poached Guavas

SERVES 4

Preparation time: 5 minutes

Cooking time: 10 minutes

*This Cape Malay recipe is quick, simple and scrumptious.*
*Yet another given to me by Karen Dudley.*

1½ cups (375 ml) white sugar
1½ cups (375 ml) water
3 x 3 cm pieces stick cinnamon
5 whole cloves
8 guavas, peeled

Dissolve the sugar in the water with the cinnamon and cloves. Boil for about 10 minutes until a syrup forms. Add the guavas whole to the syrup and poach gently for about 10 minutes, until pink.

The guavas are traditionally served with evaporated milk.

# Koeksisters

MAKES APPROXIMATELY 36

Preparation and cooking time: 1½ hours

*The recipe for this popular Afrikaans/Cape Malay confection is from Hein Walkinshaw, whom I met in a car park at Richards Bay. He makes amazing koeksisters and has been doing so for 10 years.*

| DOUGH | SYRUP |
|---|---|
| 500 g cake flour | 1 kg sugar |
| ¼ t (1 ml) salt | 2 cups (500 ml) water |
| 2 t (10 ml) baking powder | a pinch salt |
| 50 g butter | ¼ t (1.25 ml) ground ginger |
| 1 egg | 1 slice lemon, with peel |
| 1 cup (250 ml) water | vegetable oil, sufficient for deep frying |

Sift the cake flour together with the salt and baking powder. Rub in the butter with your fingers, as if making a crumble. Mix the egg and water together and slowly add it to the flour mixture, kneading it into a dough. (It is possible that not all the liquid will be necessary.) Roll the dough out to a thickness of approximately 10 mm. Cut into rectangles, approximately 8 cm x 4 cm. With kitchen scissors, slit each rectangle almost to the top to form 3 strands. Plait the strands, keeping each rectangle flat so that it doesn't stretch and remembering to pinch the plaits together at the ends. Place the plaits on a tray and cover with a slightly damp cloth.

For the syrup, mix together the sugar, water, salt, ginger and slice of lemon. Bring to the boil over a medium to high heat and leave to simmer for about 15 minutes, until it forms a syrup. Pour the syrup into a large bowl and leave to cool. Then refrigerate until cold.

Deep fry the koeksister plaits in hot oil until golden. Immediately plunge them into the cold syrup. The koeksisters will absorb the syrup. Leave to drain on a rack.

**LEFT:** *A dance club in Gordon's Bay.*

# My Mum's Cardamom and Nut Semolina

SERVES 4

Preparation time: 5 minutes

Cooking time: 15 minutes

*I remember my Mum making this dish of Indian origin for us when we were kids. I used to love it and I realized, while making it, that I hadn't eaten it for years and years. It is delicious and my friends polished it off. Once we had finished it, a friend asked if I would mind if she scraped the saucepan. So it goes down well!*

2 T (30 ml) or 40 g butter
50 g mixed nuts (e.g. almonds, cashews and walnuts), roughly chopped
50 g raisins
100 g semolina
2 cups (500 ml) milk
6 cardamom pods
100 g white sugar
fresh cream, as a topping (optional)

Melt half the butter in a pan and toss in the nuts and raisins. Brown them over a medium heat until golden, then set aside. In another pan melt the rest of the butter, add the semolina and toast for a minute or so. Pour in the milk and stir quickly. Add the cardamom pods and sugar. Lower the heat and simmer for about 15 minutes. Stir in the nuts and raisins.

Serve in little bowls with a splash of fresh cream if desired.

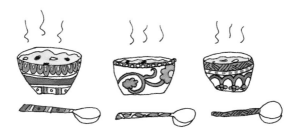

# Baked Pears in Red Wine

SERVES 4

Preparation time: 10 minutes

Cooking time: 50 minutes

*This New South African recipe was passed on to me by Karen Dudley.*

4 fat pears, de-cored (preferably with a corer)
100 g unsalted butter
1 cup (250 ml) brown sugar
8 x 3 cm pieces stick cinnamon
12 whole cloves
½ bottle (375 ml) red wine
(e.g. a South African Pinotage)

Cut the tops off the pears and put them to one side. I love this: take a knob of butter and rub it between your palms. Coat each of the pears in the butter. Place the sugar in a flattish bowl and roll the buttered pears in the sugar. Push 2 cinnamon sticks and about 3 or 4 cloves into the cavity of each pear. Replace the tops of the pears and place the pears upright in a dish. Pour the wine down the side of the dish and bake at 180 °C, keeping the pears covered with foil for the first 40 minutes and uncovered for another 10 minutes to allow the pears to become crispy.

For maximum enjoyment, serve with fresh cream.

*Baking*

# Aunty Bluma's Chocolate Cake

SERVES 6

Preparation time: 25 minutes

Cooking time: 45–50 minutes

*This recipe, of Jewish origin, is famous around Cape Town and has mutated into various other cakes.*
*However, there is only one Aunty Bluma's chocolate cake and this is it. Follow the recipe exactly*
*and do not be tempted to stray, as it is a wonderful cake.*

100 g good quality dark chocolate,
broken into pieces
5 t (25 ml) cold water
8 t (40 ml) cocoa powder
1½ cups (375 ml) white sugar
1 T (15 ml) cognac or brandy
250 g butter, cut into small blocks
4 eggs, separated
250 g self-raising flour
1 t (5 ml) icing sugar
1 small fresh edible flower

Melt the chocolate in a saucepan over a low flame, simultaneously stirring in the water, cocoa and sugar. When the mixture is smooth, remove it from the stove. Add the brandy or cognac, then the butter and stir well, allowing it to melt. Remove from heat and when cool, stir in the egg yolks and flour thoroughly. Beat the egg whites until stiff and fold them into the mixture. Pour the mixture in a greased cake tin and bake in the oven at 180 °C for 45–50 minutes. Turn out onto a wire rack and when cool, sieve the icing sugar over the cake. You can make it look pretty by placing a flower on top.

**LEFT:** *En route to the District Six Museum, I parked my car and saw this most beautiful building. Beinkinstadt's, the Jewish Bookshop, Canterbury Street, Cape Town.*

# Splashy Fen Cheese Scones

MAKES 8 SCONES

Preparation time: 10 minutes

Cooking time: 15 minutes

*This is an English recipe from Peter Ferraz of the Splashy Fen farm in KwaZulu-Natal, venue of the annual folk music festival. Peter says that the recipe comes from his grandmother but she claims that it comes from him! Either way, the scones are simple to make and most delicious.*

1 cup (120 g) flour
1 cup (100 g) grated Cheddar cheese
1 t (5 ml) baking powder
1 t (5 ml) salt
⅔ cup (160 ml) milk

Lightly mix the flour, cheese, baking powder and salt together. Stir in the milk with a spoon. Drop dollops of the mixture onto a greased baking tray. (Peter was adamant that they should be dollops and not shaped rounds.) Bake them in the oven at 220 °C for 15–20 minutes, or until the tops are nicely browned.

Serve while still warm, with a sliver of butter spread into each – a wonderful mid-Sunday morning treat.

# Mrs Beukes' Barrydale Tipsy Tart

SERVES 6

Preparation time: 20 minutes

Cooking time: 30–40 minutes

*I am very grateful to Mrs Beukes for this popular Afrikaans recipe. It is very simple and totally delicious.*

1 t (5 ml) bicarbonate of soda
1 cup (250 ml) boiling water
250 g dates, pitted and sliced in small pieces
125 g margarine
1 cup (250 ml) white sugar
2 eggs
2 cups (240 g) white flour
1 t (5 ml) baking powder
a pinch salt
250 g chopped pecan nuts or walnuts

SYRUP
1¼ cups (310 ml) white sugar
1 T (15 ml) margarine
⅓ cup (80 ml) water
1 t (5 ml) vanilla essence
a pinch salt
½ cup (125 ml) brandy

Preheat the oven to 180 °C. Mix the bicarbonate of soda and boiling water in a bowl with half the dates. Stir well and leave to cool. Beat the margarine and sugar together until smooth. Mix in the eggs to form a paste. Sift the flour, baking powder and salt into the mixture, then add nuts and remaining dates. Stir in the date and bicarbonate of soda mixture. Pour into a greased cake tin and bake for 30–40 minutes.

Boil the sugar, margarine and water over a medium heat, for about 5 minutes. Remove from the heat and add vanilla essence, salt and brandy. Pour this syrup over the tart and serve hot or cold with fresh cream.

# Lemon Squares

MAKES APPROXIMATELY 12 LARGE SQUARES
Preparation time: 25 minutes
Cooking time: 50–55 minutes

*The New South African recipe for these delicious lemon squares comes from Karen Dudley.*

SHORTBREAD
125 g softened butter
150 g cake flour
75 g icing sugar
¼ t (1 ml) lemon essence

TOPPING
2 eggs
1 cup (250 ml) sugar
¼ t (1 ml) lemon essence
juice and zest (finely grated peel) of 1 lemon
4 T (30 g or 60 ml) flour
½ t (2.5 ml) baking powder
icing sugar, for dusting

Combine the butter, flour, icing sugar and lemon essence in a food processor until it forms a ball. Press the dough evenly into a greased baking tray, approximately 16 cm x 16 cm. Bake for 20 minutes, or until golden, at 180 °C.

For the topping, beat the eggs well and add the sugar until the mixture is thick and pale yellow. Gradually add the lemon essence, lemon juice and zest, flour and baking powder. When the shortbread is golden, take it out and pour the lemon mixture over the crust. Return it to the oven and bake at 160 °C for a further 30–35 minutes (golden on top). Once cool, cut into squares, remove from pan and dust with icing sugar. You can also use templates, such as hearts and stars, and dust the shapes onto the squares.

LEFT: *Rose's tidy shelves.*

# Melk Tert

SERVES 4–6
Preparation time: 40 minutes
Cooking time: ± 30 minutes

*This traditional Afrikaans milk tart recipe was given to me by my Aunt Elaine.*

| PIE SHELL | FILLING |
|---|---|
| 50 g butter | 2 cups (500 ml) milk |
| 50 g white sugar | ½ T (7.5 ml) butter |
| 1 egg | 4 t (20 ml) cake flour |
| 100 g cake flour | 4 t (20 ml) cornflour |
| 1 t (5 ml) baking powder | ½ cup (125 ml) sugar |
| a pinch salt | 1 egg |
| ceramic baking beads or dried red kidney beans | 1 T (15 ml) vanilla essence |
| | a pinch ground cinnamon |

Preheat the oven to 200 °C and grease a 23 cm pie tin. Cream the butter and sugar together, then mix in the egg. Sieve in the flour, baking powder and salt. Mix well, then knead by hand into a dough. Roll it out and line a pie tin. Place oiled foil or greaseproof paper onto the pastry and weigh it down with baking beads or kidney beans. Blind bake this for 10 minutes. Remove the foil/paper and bake for another 5 minutes. Allow the shell to cool.

Boil the milk and butter over a moderate heat. Mix the flour, cornflour, sugar and egg to a paste, then add the vanilla essence. Add this to the milk and stir until the custard thickens. Once stiff, pour into the pastry shell. Sprinkle with cinnamon and serve with fresh cream.

# Aartappel Porring
# (Potato Pudding with Stewed Fruit)

SERVES 6

Preparation time: 25 minutes

Cooking time: 20 minutes

*This unusual but tasty Cape Malay recipe is delicious served with fresh cream. It comes from Lutfia Boran.*

6 medium to large potatoes,
peeled and chopped

400 g butter

¾ cup (185 ml) sugar

½ t (2.5 ml) lemon essence

½ t (2.5 ml) almond essence

4 eggs

200 g mixed dried fruit

½ cup (125 ml) sugar

2 x 3 cm pieces stick cinnamon

1 cup (250 ml) water

Boil the potatoes, then drain and mash them with butter and sugar. Add the lemon and almond essences. Mix in the eggs. Bake in an ovenproof dish at 180 °C for 20 minutes.

In the meantime, prepare the stewed fruit. Place the dried fruit, sugar, cinnamon and water in a saucepan and bring to the boil, then reduce heat and simmer for about 15–20 minutes, adding more water if necessary.

Serve the potato pudding topped with the stewed fruit and a dash of cream.

# Index